We Are
Fearless
Queens

KILLER CLAPBACKS FROM
100 MODERN ICONS

POP PRESS

Pop Press, an imprint of Ebury Publishing,
20 Vauxhall Bridge Road,
London, SW1V 2SA

Pop Press is part of the Penguin Random House group of companies
whose addresses can be found at global.penguinrandomhouse.com

Penguin
Random House
UK

First published by Pop Press in 2021

www.penguin.co.uk

A CIP catalogue record for this book is available from the British Library

Design: Seagull Design
Text: Grace Paul
Illustrations: Ellie Forster

ISBN: 9781529109139

Typeset in 11/14 pt Beton Std
by Integra Software Services Pvt. Ltd, Pondicherry

Printed and bound in Printed and bound in
Great Britain by Clays Ltd, Elcograf S.p.A.

The authorised representative in the EEA is Penguin Random House Ireland,
Morrison Chambers, 32 Nassau Street, Dublin D02 YH68.

Penguin Random House is committed to a sustainable future for
our business, our readers and our planet. This book is made from
Forest Stewardship Council® certified paper.

MIX
Paper from
responsible sources
FSC® C018179
FSC
www.fsc.org

Contents

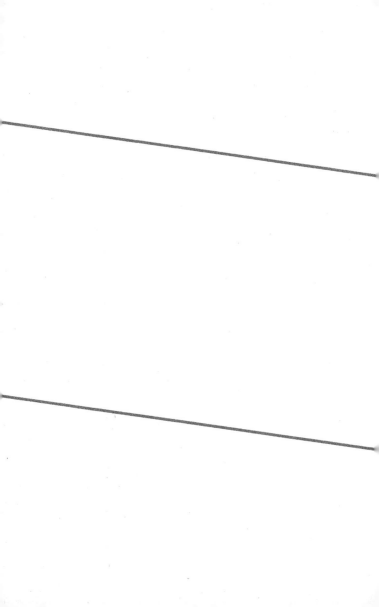

Be a
fearless
Queen

Be a fearless Queen

They say that no question is a stupid question, but sometimes women find themselves at the end of the stupidest ones: Can you smile more? When are you going to have kids? Are you looking for a partner right now then? What's your diet regime? Questions that get you thinking, 'Would you ask a man the same thing?'

The women within this book will show you how to clap back to such questions with aplomb, slamming patriarchy in the face by uttering epic retorts that leave their opponents open-mouthed and people around the world applauding them. Learn from them as it's time to stand up and clap back, ladies.

They'll also teach you how to empower yourself in all areas of your lives, from your careers to demanding more money, to body positivity and equality. They've got it covered, providing us with IDGAF badassery that we all need a little more of.

Remember: don't try to challenge us, we are fearless queens.

10 rules to be the Queen of your own life

To be a fearless queen, who slays on a daily basis, you need to look after number one first. If you can't treat yourself with respect, how the hell can you treat others the same way?

- Look after yourself.

- Treat yourself with compassion.

- Know your worth.

- Make yourself vulnerable.

- Don't compare.

- Set boundaries.

- Embrace failure.

- Be resilient.

- Take risks.

- Lift as you climb.

Billie Eilish

Career

'Smiling doesn't win
you gold medals.'

SIMONE BILES AFTER BEING ASKED
WHY SHE WASN'T SMILING AT BEING
COMPLIMENTED DURING *DANCING WITH
THE STARS*

'Some women choose to follow men, and some women choose to follow their dreams. If you're wondering which way to go, remember that your career will never wake up and tell you that it doesn't love you anymore.'

LADY GAGA

'Don't let people tell you
that you're too old.
That it's over, 'cause
that's a lie.'

JADA PINKETT SMITH

'Um, I actually was trained in calculus for several years. I'm a neuroscientist.'

MAYIM BIALIK WHEN ASKED IF SHE CAN SOLVE MATHS PROBLEMS

'The only thing that separates women of color from anyone else is opportunity.'

VIOLA DAVIES

'Actually being able to exercise your own choice can bring about greater opportunity. I think it's just as important what you say no to as what you say yes to.'

SANDRA OH

'Everyone should be sacked at least once in their career, because perfection doesn't exist.'

ANNA WINTOUR

'I just love bossy women. I could be around them all day. To me, bossy is not a pejorative term at all. It means somebody's passionate and engaged and ambitious and doesn't mind leading.'

AMY POEHLER

'Are you going to ask all
the men that tonight?'

KIERA KNIGHTLEY AFTER BEING ASKED
HOW SHE BALANCES HER CAREER AND
PERSONAL LIFE AT THE HOLLYWOOD
FILM AWARDS

'You don't have to force your career to happen all at once.'

AMANDLA STENBERG

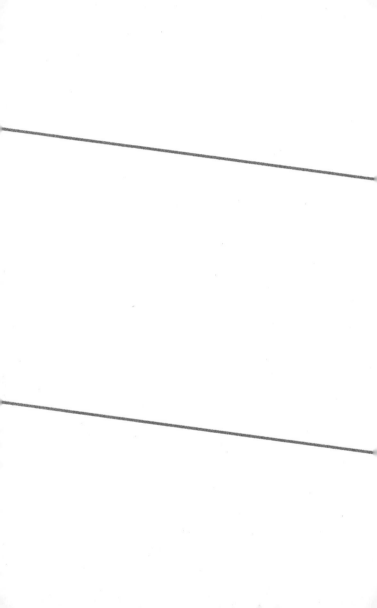

Money

'I do think women need
to talk about money
more often.'

REESE WITHERSPOON

'A guy wouldn't have any problem asking for $600,000 an episode. And as women, we're like, "Oh, can I ask for that? Is that OK?"'

ELLEN POMPEO

'I'm not taking jobs
anymore where I'm
getting paid a quarter
of what the male co-star
is being paid. I'm not
allowing that in my life.'

JESSICA CHASTAIN

'I still believe that women should get paid equal and should be treated with respect. I'm all about that.'

DOLLY PARTON

'My mum said to me,
"You know, sweetheart,
one day you should settle
down and marry a rich
man." I said, "Mum, I am
a rich man."'

CHER

'I gotta tell myself, '"Stop feeling guilty. You worked for this."'

CARDI B ON HOW SHE FEELS GUILTY
ABOUT SPENDING MONEY SOMETIMES

'My goal is to make sure that all women of colour get equal pay, and all women get equal pay.'

OCTAVIA SPENCER

'A man is still getting paid more money to do the same job as a woman does, in Hollywood and everywhere else. And no matter where you live or what you do, that's bullsh*t.'

JUDY GREER

'Part of the reason I don't worry about what other people think about me is because I know that even if I lose all my money and my job and my opportunities tomorrow, I'm very capable of creating meaning without all of the stuff around.'

CONSTANCE WU

'Don't spend it,
invest it.'

SERENA WILLIAMS

Dua Lipa

Confidence

'I'm not going to let anybody mould me, even though many people have attempted to.'

LETITIA WRIGHT

'Women don't need to
find their voice. They
need to feel empowered
to use it and people need
to be encouraged
to listen.'

MEGHAN MARKLE

'We need strong women that are willing to say what they have to say, even when they're getting backlash for it.'

NICKI MINAJ

'Sometimes you have to be bold and keep repeating yourself to normalise things.'

HAYLEY KIYOKO

'The most important thing
is to be authentic.'

DUA LIPA

'We need people who think outside the box and who aren't like everyone else.'

GRETA THUNBERG

'You gotta believe in yourself. Because there are going to be times that people tell you [that] you can't do it or you don't look the part. But I am a walking testimony.'

MISSY ELLIOTT

'If there's anyone out there who looks like me or feels out of place trying to get into performing and all this kind of stuff, say, "You are beautiful – embrace it; you are intelligent – embrace it; you are powerful – embrace it."'

MICHAELA COEL

'In all of our lives, all of us will experience people who try to tell us who to be and what to be. F*ck those people!'

MILEY CYRUS

'When I came out of
my mother's womb, I
screamed "Girl Power".'

GERI HALLIWELL

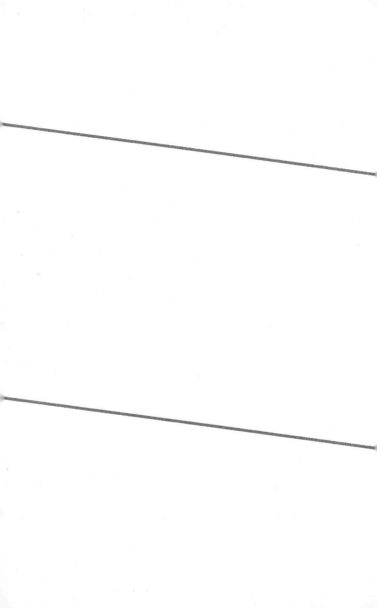

Body
positivity

'I would like to put airbrushing in the bin. I want it gone. I want it out of here.'

JAMEELA JAMIL

'If anybody even tries to whisper the word diet, I'm like, "You can go fuck yourself."'

JENNIFER LAWRENCE

'Instead of thinking,
"Am I skinny?" I grew
up thinking, "Am I fast
enough? How can I use
my body?"'

PINK

'Are you trying to lose weight? Like, what's the deal, man? You look great. [...] Seriously, we have to talk about this ... Are you trying to fit into a catsuit?'

ANNE HATHAWAY ON BEING REPEATEDLY ASKED ABOUT HER 'FORMFITTING' CATWOMAN SUIT

'For me, body hair is another opportunity for women to exercise their ability to choose – a choice based on how they want to feel and their associations with having or not having body hair.'

EMILY RATAJKOWSKI

'I am not a woman whose self-worth comes from her dress size.'

KRISTEN BELL

'My body is mine and yours is yours. Our own bodies are kind of the only real things which are truly ours. I get to see it and get to show it when I want to.'

BILLIE EILISH

'No means no. That's it.
It doesn't matter how far
I take it or what I have
on, when I say no.
It means no.'

AMBER ROSE

'I've never seen
magazines or music
videos and been like,
"I need to look like that to
be a success."'

ADELE

'Why do you get, like,
the really interesting,
existential questions, and
I get the, like, rabbit
food question?'

SCARLETT JOHANSSON TO HER MALE
CO-STAR WHEN SHE WAS ASKED BY AN
INTERVIEWER ABOUT HER DIET

Lizzo

Beauty

'The key to beauty is the inside job.'

ALEXANDRIA OCASIO-CORTEZ

'I'm wearing Ede & Ravenscroft.'

AMAL CLOONEY ON BEING ASKED
WHAT SHE'S WEARING WHILST SHE WAS
REPRESENTING ARMENIA IN THE EUROPEAN
COURT OF HUMAN RIGHTS – SHE REFERRED
TO THE BRAND OF HER LEGAL ROBES

'I'm happy that this is the
face that God gave me,
and it's imperfect.'

LAVERNE COX

'If the way I look
displeases you, that's your
problem, not mine.'

IRIS APFEL

'My greatest beauty secret
is being happy with
myself. It's a mistake to
think you are what you
put on yourself. I believe
that a lot of how you look
has to do with how you
feel about yourself and
your life.'

TINA TURNER

'If you retain nothing
else, always remember the
most important rule
of beauty, which is:
who cares?'

TINA FEY

'Find things that suit you. That's how you look extraordinary.'

VIVIENNE WESTWOOD

'Who is the beauty icon that inspires you the most? Is it Sophia Loren? Audrey Hepburn? Halle Berry? Mine is Nosferatu, because that vampire taught me my number one and number two favourite beauty tricks of all time: avoid the sun at all costs and always try to appear shrouded in shadows.'

MINDY KALING

'For me, hair is a physical manifestation of my self-confidence. So the more comfortable I become, the bigger my hair gets.'

CIPRIANA QUANN

'Vivienne Westwood, Tom Ford shoes and an o.b. tampon.'

AMY SCHUMER ON BEING ASKED WHAT SHE'S WEARING ON THE RED CARPET

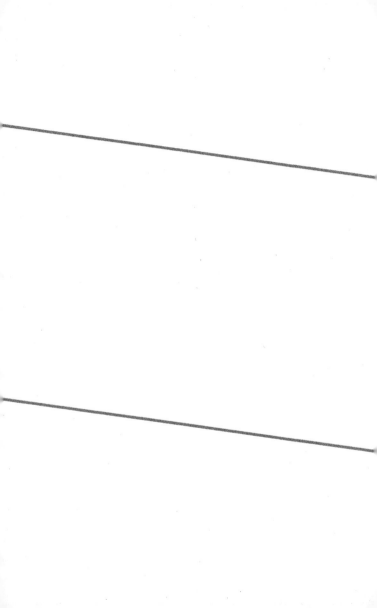

Mental
health

'Most women on meds
are women who have
been brave enough to
help themselves.'

LENA DUNHAM

'My brain and my heart
are really important to
me. I don't know why
I wouldn't seek help to
have those things be as
healthy as my teeth. I go
to the dentist. So why
wouldn't I go to a shrink?'

KERRY WASHINGTON

'Knowing that a lot of my fears are not reality-based really helps.'

AMANDA SEYFRIED

'I wish more people would talk about therapy. We girls, we're taught to be almost too resilient, to be strong and sexy and cool and laid-back, the girl who's down. We also need to feel allowed to fall apart.'

SELENA GOMEZ

'Being vulnerable is actually a strength and not a weakness – that's why more and more mental health is such an important thing to talk about.'

CARA DELEVINGNE

'There was something hurting inside me, and I didn't have the skill to heal it or handle it. In order to heal it, I had to talk about it.'

CAMILA CABELLO

'It's time to tell everyone who's dealing with a mental health issue that they're not alone, and that getting support and treatment isn't a sign of weakness, it's a sign of strength.'

MICHELLE OBAMA

'The tough times, the days when you're just a ball on the floor – they'll pass. You're playing the long game and life is totally worth it.'

SARAH SILVERMAN

'It's hard to remain sad
if you're focused on
what you have instead
of what you don't have.'

OPRAH WINFREY

'It's not because I'm
oversensitive. It's not
because I take it to heart.
It's not because I'm
overdramatic. It's because
I have a mental illness.'

HALSEY

Munroe Bergdorf

Resilience

'I learned that, in the face of a void or in the face of any challenge, you can choose joy and meaning.'

SHERYL SANDBERG

'You can recognize very often that out of these projects that may not have succeeded themselves that other successes are built.'

ARIANNA HUFFINGTON

'Be the heroine of your story, not the victim.'

NORA EPHRON

'If I could go back and give myself advice, I'd say "Don't be so nervous about everything".'

MAGGIE SMITH

'When you fall down –
which you have to [do] if
you want to learn to be a
skater – you pick yourself
right up and start again.'

VERA WANG

'You're never too good
to lose; you're never too
big to lose.'

BEYONCÉ

'You've got to experience failure to understand that you can survive it.'

TINA FEY

'Facing rejection day after day can be really, really tough ... It is funny how the things that happen in your life can feel terrible in the moment but lead you to those [successful] places.'

EMMA STONE

'If you feel like you don't have anybody, look within yourself and try to find that resilience that will ultimately get you through whatever it is you're going through.'

DEMI LOVATO

'I really believe there is a possibility of growth with pain. I am a thousand times more interesting as a person having gone through that – and more useful as a person.'

HELENA BONHAM CARTER

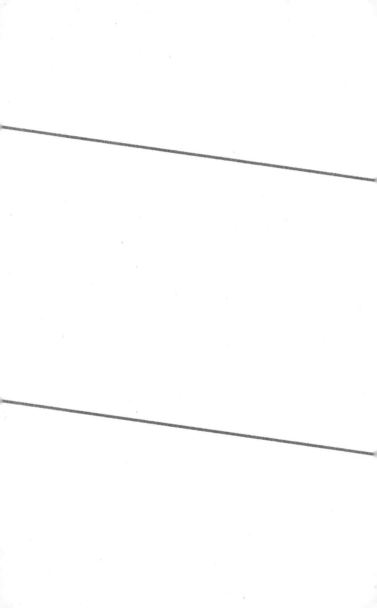

Equality

'Feminist: the person who believes in the social, political, and economic equality of the sexes.'

CHIMAMANDA NGOZI ADICHIE

'You have as much right to be there as anybody else with any other kind of background.'

JODIE COMER

'We just need to be allowing people to be who they are.'

MUNROE BERGDORF

'Feminism is just another word for equality. It means equality and no one would object equality and no one should object equality and it just means that women should have equal rights as men.'

MALALA YOUSAFZAI

'The lack of inclusion for women in decision-making in every single institution in the world makes me angry. Why are the people making those decisions not half women? That seems wrong to me.'

MERYL STREEP

'Only you know who you
were born to be, and
you need to be free to
be that person.'

RUBY ROSE

'I don't want people
messing with me, so
I defend everybody's
right to be themselves.
That has always been
my battle cry.'

WHOOPI GOLDBERG

'My collaborators and colleagues don't refer to me as a female writer, like, "Can you send in your latest female draft of that, please?"'

PHOEBE WALLER-BRIDGE ON HOW HER GENDER BECOMES RELEVANT WHEN SHE'S DOING PRESS

'Allyship is so much deeper than just being cool with someone's life or cool with someone's existence, it's about reaching out a hand and pulling them up and making sure that ya'll are walking side by side.'

LIZZO

'Is this what you think girls have trouble choosing between? Is this men assuming that that's what girls would have to choose between?'

ARIANA GRANDE WHEN ASKED IF SHE COULD PICK BETWEEN USING MAKEUP OR HER PHONE ONE LAST TIME

Adele

Relationships

'CEO.'

LAUREN CONRAD ON BEING ASKED WHAT
HER FAVOURITE SEX POSITION IS

'I will talk about being gay till the sun comes up.'

KING PRINCESS

'I'm the chooser, and
I can choose to get
married if I want to.
But in the meantime,
I am choicefully single.
Happily, gloriously
single.'

TRACEE ELLIS ROSS

'We push away the ones that really want to love us, and that's when they become our teacher and we have to say, "What am I doing wrong here? Why am I repeating this situation?"'

MICHELLE VISAGE

'I'm not looking for a
man, let's start there.'

RIHANNA ON BEING ASKED WHAT SHE
LOOKS FOR IN A MAN

'I think love and trust and telling the truth. Never let the sun set on a quarrel.'

MIRIAM MARGOLYES ON THE SECRET TO A HAPPY RELATIONSHIP

'I'm very happy [being single]. I call it being self-partnered.'

EMMA WATSON

'Let things go where they need to go. Don't hold on because when you hold on you kill love.'

WILLOW SMITH

'I'm not going to walk home with any men tonight ... I'm going to go hang out with my friends and them go home to the cats.'

TAYLOR SWIFT AFTER BEING ASKED WHICH MAN SHE WOULD BE GOING HOME WITH THAT NIGHT

'I think that the number one thing in any relationship is a friendship and building trust with that person'

ZENDAYA

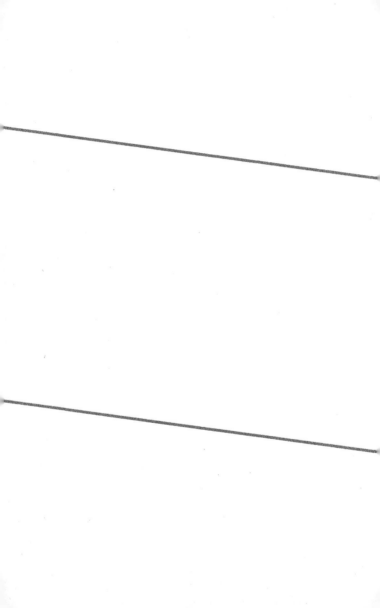

Motherhood

'You make sure your boy is the ultimate feminist, that he loves and respects women. You have to raise them to be feminists. That is our future.'

CHRISSY TEIGEN ON RAISING HER SON

'What motherhood shows
you is how selfless you
can get. I'm ragged tired.
Who cares? My kids are
healthy, I'm happy.'

MILA KUNIS

'After becoming a mother,
the amount of shit that
you get done, you're so
impressed with yourself!
It's the most empowering
feeling, because it makes
you want to worry about
the pettiness and trivial
things a lot less.'

KELLY CLARKSON

'We are complete with or without a mate, with or without a child. We get to decide for ourselves what is beautiful when it comes to our bodies. That decision is ours and ours alone.'

JENNIFER ANISTON

'I got married and
the first question in
almost every interview
is "Babies? When are
you having one?" I'm
so angry that there's this
social contract. You're
married, now have a
baby. Don't presume. I'll
do what I'm going to do.'

MARGOT ROBBIE

'You want to torture someone? Hand them an adorable baby they love who doesn't sleep.'

SHONDA RHIMES

'You're going to get advice from a lot of people and you can take bits and pieces, but you know innately what your child needs. You should trust that.'

LUCY LIU

'Now that you can finally confirm that she [her vagina] is, in fact, still there, she isn't the gal that you remember – and would rather you back off and give her some space (and an ice diaper) for the time being, thank you very much.'

OLIVIA WILDE ON THE FIRST WEEKS OF MOTHERHOOD

'Like all parents, my husband and I just do the best we can, hold our breath and hope we've set aside enough money for our kids' therapy.'

MICHELLE PFEIFFER

'Every day is such a learning experience – they [children] challenge you in so many ways.'

EVA MENDES

Acknowledgements

p6 from *Washington Post*, '"Smiling doesn't win you gold medals": Simone Biles has the perfect comeback on "DWTS"' (2017), p7 from *Cosmopolitan*, 'Lady Gaga Wants You' (2010), p8 from *Harper's Bazaar*, 'The New American Dynasty' (2018), p9 from TNT interview (2014), p10 from *The Atlantic*, 'The Emmys Speech of the Night' (2015), p11 from *Vanity Fair*, 'Sandra Oh's Been Waiting 30 Years for a Show Like *Killing Eve*' (2018), p12 from *Winners and How They Succeed* (2015), p13 from *Glamour*, 'Amy Poehler Tells Katie Couric, "I Just Love Bossy Women"' (2011), p14 from Hollywood Film Awards interview (2014), p18 from CBC, '5 Things You Should Probably Know About Amandla Stenberg' (2018), p18 from BuzzFeed Celeb interview (2020), p19 from *The Hollywood Reporter* 'Ellen Pompeo, TV's $20 Million Woman, Reveals Her Behind-the-Scenes Fight for "What I Deserve"' (2018), p20 from *Variety*, 'How Jessica Chastain Negotiates for Equal Pay' (2017), p21 from ABC News interview (2019), p22 from Dateline NBC interview (1996), p23 from *Fader*, 'Cardi B Did it Her Way' (2017), p24 from Hollywood Foreign Press Association's 'Women Breaking Barriers: Where Are We Now?' panel (2019), p25 from *Glamour*, 'Actress Judy Greer: Why Should a Man Make More Than Me?' (2015), p26 from *Vulture*, 'Constance Wu Doesn't Want to Be Your "It" Girl' (2016), p27 from *People*, 'Serena Williams Reveals She's a "Boring Spender": "I Am Really Bad at Treating Myself"' (2020), p30 from *Evening Standard*, 'Letitia Wright on how she's taking charge of her own future' (2018), p31 from *Elle*, 'Meghan Markle Addresses #MeToo, Time's Up And Encourages Women to Use Their Voices' (2018), p32 from *Variety*, 'Nicky Minaj Sheds Tears for Koba, Cheers for Larry David in Unfiltered Q&A' (2020), p33 from the *Evening Standard*, 'Hayley Kiyoko interview' (2019), p34 from *Vogue*, '"It's important to me to show unity between women" – Dua Lipa's Quest to Produce Music That Matters' (2020), p35 from CBS *This Morning* interview (2019), p36 from ESSENCE, 'Missy Elliott Delivered A Word During The 2018 ESSENCE Black Women in Music Event' (2018), p37 from Batta TV Awards 2016 speech, p38 from Rock and Roll Hall of Fame speech (2015), p39 from *Egos & Icons* interview (1999), p42 from BBC News, 'Viewpoint: Jameela Jamil on Why Airbrushing Should Be Illegal' (2018), p43 from the *Guardian*, 'Jennifer Lawrence "Told to Diet" to Save Career' (2013), p44 from *Who Magazine*, 'Pink Stripped Bare' (2014), p45 from Extra TV interview (2012), p46 from *Harper's Bazaar* 'Emily Ratajkowski Explores What It Means to Be Hyper Feminine' (2019), p47 from *Redbook Magazine*, 'How to Be Happy, by Kristen Bell' (2013), p48 from *GQ Magazine*, 'Billie Eilish: Confessions of a Teenage Superstar' (2020), p49 from *It's Not You, It's Men* (2016), p50 from Cool Convo interview (2013), p51 from *Avengers* UK press conference (2012), p54 from *Vogue*, 'Congresswoman Alexandria Ocasio-Cortez's Guide to Her Signature Red Lip' (2020), p55 from the *Telegraph* interview (2015), p56 from the *Guardian*, 'Laverne Cox: "Now I Have The Money to Feminise My Face I Don't Want To. I'm Happy That This Is The Face That God Gave Me"' (2015), p57 from *Slutever*, 'I Got Beauty Advice from Iris Apfel' (2015), p58 from *Woman and Home Magazine*, 'Tina Turner's Top Secrets' (2016), p59 from *Bossypants* (2011), p60 from Miss Vogue, 'Vivienne Westwood Is The Modern It Girl's Label Of Choice' (2019), p61 from *Why Not Me?* (2015), p62 from Into the Gloss, 'Cipriana and TK Quann, Urban Bush Babes' (2015), p63 from E! News interview (2016), p66 from *Vulture*, 'Lena Dunham Explains How Her Anxiety Is Different From Hannah's' (2017), p67 from *Glamour*, 'Michelle Obama, Sarah Jessica Parker, and Kerry Washington: The Important Cause Bringing Three Powerhouse Women Together' (2015), p68 from *Allure*, 'Amanda Seyfried on Her Mental Health, Her Dog and Those Eyes' (2016), p69 from *Vogue*, 'Selena Gomez on Instagram Fatigue, Good Mental Health, and Stepping Back From the Limelight' (2017), p70 from *This Morning* interview (2017), p71 from *WSJ Magazine*, 'How Camila Cabello Became Friends With Her Anxiety (2020), p72 from 'Change Direction' Mental Health Event (2015), p73 from *Glamour*, 'Sarah Silverman Opens Up About Her Battle with Depression and Her Gutsiest Career Move Yet' (2015), p74 from *Vogue*, 'Oprah Winfrey Is on a Roll Again' (2017), p75 from Pedestrian TV interview (2016), p78 from *Elle*, 'Addressing Graduates, Sheryl Sandberg Reflects On The Lessons That Grief Teaches' (2016), *Building Resilience, and Finding Joy* (2017), p79 from CNN, 'Arianna Huffington tells women: "Less stress, more living"' (2013), p80 from Wellesley College Commencement 1996 speech (1996), p81 from the *Ritz Magazine*, 'Taking the Lead: An Interview with Film Icon Maggie Smith' (2016), p82 from The Business of Fashion, 'Vera Wang Says Keep Your Feet on the Ground and Don't Get Ahead of Yourself' (2013), p83 from 'Self-Titled: Part 2. Imperfection' video (2013), p84 from *Seventeen*, 'Funny Girl' (2008), p85 from *Teen Vogue*, 'Emma Stone, Ryan Gosling Remember Early Career Struggles' (2016), p86 from *Dr Phil* interview (2018), p87 from *The Times*, 'Helena Bonham Carter Interview' (2019), p90 from *We All Should be Feminists* (2014), p91 from *Glamour*, 'I don't want to be anyone's cup of milky teal' Jodie Comer on her perfect brew for dealing with classism & her beauty regime' (2020), p92 from *Glamour*, 'Munroe Bergdort: "As A Person Of Colour, A Trans Person, A Queer Person and As A Woman, I've Been Navigating a Hostile Environment My Whole Life"' (2020), p93 from World Economic Forum interview (2018) and Dealing with Her Emotional Scars' (2019), p94 from the *Suffragette* Press Conference (2015), p95 from *Elle*, 'OITNB's Ruby Rose Schools Us On Gender Fluidity' (2015), p96 from Between the Lines, 'Whoopi Goldberg Q&A' (2014), p97 from Deadline, 'Phoebe Waller-Bridge On Bringing Bond Into The Present, Why Femaleness Can't Be Categorized & The New Project That Came To Her In A Dream' (2019), p98 from *Junkee*, 'Lizzo is About to Conquer the World, So You'd Better Listen Up' (2019), p99 from Power 106 FM interview (2015), p102 from SiriusXM interview (2012), p103 from *Vulture*, 'Bend the Knee: King Princess, Brooklyn Queer Pop Royalty, Is Ready For The throne', (2019), p104 from Oprah's 2020 Vision Tour Visionaries interview (2020), p105 from *Vice*, 'Michelle Visage Did My Make-Up and Sorted My Life Out' (2017), p106 from the Rogue Man launch interview (2014), p107 from the *Guardian*, 'Miriam Margolyes: "I like men – I just don't feel groin excitement"' (2020), p108 from *Vogue*, 'From The Archive: Emma Watson On Being Happily "Self-Partnered" At 30' (2019), p109 from The Fader, 'Willow Smith's Almost-Grown Angst' (2017), p110 from *Entertainment Tonight* interview (2015), P111 from *Teen Vogue* (2017) p114 from *Glamour*, '"It's Quite a Story"' (2020), p115 from *Marie Claire*, 'Mila Kunis Is Like It (Actually) Is' (2017), p116 from Refinery29, 'Kelly Clarkson tells R29 The Lesson it Took Her 15 Years to Learn' (2017), p117 from *Huffington Post*, 'For the Record' (2016), p118 from the *Radio Times*, 'Margot Robbie is Developing a TV Series About Female WWII Codebreakers' (2019), p119 from *Motherwell*, 'Shonda Rhimes On The Greeting Cards Mothers Really Need' (2017), p120 from *Today*, 'Lucy Liu Opens Up About Becoming a Mom' (2016), p121 from *Shape*, 'Olivia Wilde Gets Real About Her Body After Baby' (2015), p122 from *Closer Weekly*, 'Michelle Pfeiffer Reveals the Best Advice She Ever Received From Her Mother' (2019), p123 from *Women's Health Magazine*, 'Eva Mendes: "I Didn't See Myself As A Mother – Until I Met Ryan"' (2019)